How Do They Grow?

From Lamb to Sheep

by Jillian Powell

HODDER
Wayland

an imprint of Hodder Children's Books

© 2001 White-Thomson Publishing Ltd

Produced for Hodder Wayland by
White-Thomson Publishing Ltd
2/3 St. Andrew's Place
Lewes, East Sussex
BN7 1UP

Editor: Sarah Doughty
Designer: Tessa Barwick
Text consultant: Jessica Buss
Language consultant: Norah Granger

Published in Great Britain in 2001 by Hodder Wayland,
an imprint of Hodder Children's Books.

British Library Cataloguing in Publication Data
    Powell, Jillian
        From Lamb to Sheep. – (How do they Grow?)
        1. Lambs – Development – Juvenile literature 2. Sheep –
        Physiology – Juvenile literature
        I. Title
        636.3

ISBN 0 7502 2677 3

Printed and bound in Italy by G.Canale & C.S.p.A.

Hodder Children's Books
A division of Hodder Headline Ltd
338 Euston Road, London NW1 3BH

Contents

Lambing time 4

The newborn lamb 6

Starting to feed 8

Lambs' tails 10

Feeding the lambs 12

Telling the lambs apart 14

Special food 16

Drinking and grazing 18

Healthy lambs 20

Weighing the lambs 22

Ready to be sold 24

Ewes and rams for breeding 26

Having lambs 28

Glossary 30

Further information 31

Index 32

Words in **bold** in the text can be found in the glossary on page 30.

Lambing time

These **ewes** are in a lambing shed, ready to give birth. Most lambs are born in the early springtime.

A ewe often gives birth lying down. The lamb's nose and front legs appear first.

The newborn lamb

The lamb is born.
Its coat is wet.
The ewe licks it
to clean and dry it
and to keep the lamb warm.

The lamb tries to stand up but its legs are wobbly. The lamb is hungry and wants to drink its mother's milk.

Starting to feed

This lamb is drinking milk. Milk helps it to grow strong and fight off **germs**. Lambs feed on their mother's milk for about 12 weeks.

This lamb is being fed milk from a bottle.
Lambs are fed in this way if their mothers are
not able to feed them.

Lambs' tails

Lambs are born with long tails. Their tails can pick up dirt and germs when they are out in the fields.

These lambs have had their tails made shorter. This is called **docking**. A farmer often docks the tails to help keep the **flock** healthy.

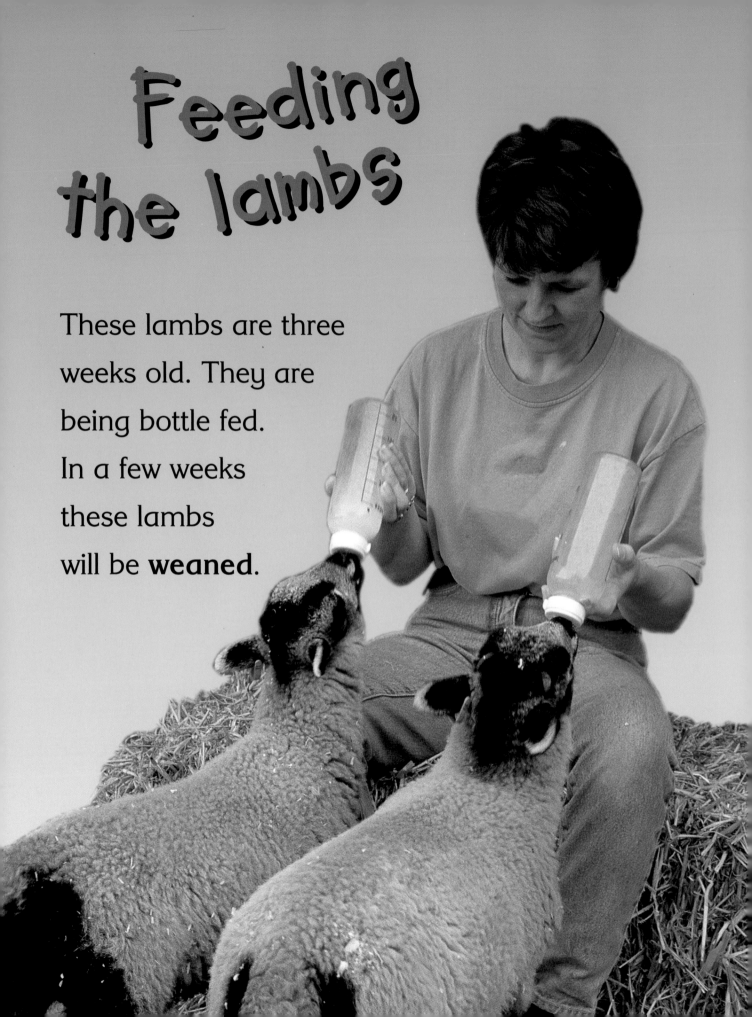

Feeding the lambs

These lambs are three weeks old. They are being bottle fed. In a few weeks these lambs will be **weaned**.

After they are weaned, the farm worker puts the lambs into a **pen** where they can eat grass.

Telling the lambs apart

The farm worker puts a **tag** in each lamb's ear. This has a number that helps the farmer to tell the lambs apart when they are out in the fields.

She puts a mark on the lambs' coats so they can be matched up with their mothers or their brothers and sisters.

Special food

These lambs are three months old and growing fast. The lambs eat their food from a **trough**. The mixture is a dry food made of **grains**.

The lambs eat hay from a hay rack.
Hay is grass that has been
dried by the sun.

Drinking and grazing

The lambs need to drink water
every day. This lamb is
drinking clean water from
a trough in the field.

The lambs **graze** in the fresh grass. They pull
at the grass and chew it until it is soft enough
to swallow.

Healthy lambs

A vet checks all the lambs to make sure they are healthy. He checks that there are no problems with each lamb's teeth or its feet.

Lambs are given **medicine** to stop them getting **worms** or diseases.

Weighing the lambs

These lambs have grown bigger and heavier.
Their wool coats are longer and thicker.

When they were born, the lambs weighed about 4.5 kg. At four months old, they weigh between 32 kg and 40 kg.

Ready to be sold

These lambs are ready to be sold.
They are loaded on to a truck which will take
them to a **livestock market**.

Some lambs are sold for meat. Others stay on the sheep farm for breeding. This means more lambs will be born every year.

Ewes and rams for breeding

Lambs kept for breeding stay on the farm with the older sheep. When a ewe is in her second year she is ready to **mate**.

The farmer keeps a **ram** to mate with the ewes.
After they have mated, some of the ewes will
have baby lambs growing inside them.

Having lambs

The ewes carry the tiny baby lambs inside their bodies for five months. A ewe may give birth to one, two or three lambs.

When her lambs are born, the ewe feeds and looks after them. Like her, they will grow up to be strong and healthy sheep.

Glossary

Docking Making an animal's tail shorter.

Ewes Female sheep.

Flock A large group of animals, such as sheep.

Germs Tiny particles around us that can carry disease.

Grains The seeds of a cereal crop.

Graze To feed on grass.

Livestock market A place where farmers can meet to buy and sell animals.

Mate When a male and female come together to have babies. A male gives a female a seed which makes a female egg grow into a baby animal.

Medicine Drugs that are taken to avoid illness or disease.

Pen An enclosed area where animals can be safely kept.

Ram A male sheep.

Tag A label that gives something a name, number or identity.

Trough A long container that holds food or water for farm animals.

Weaned When an animal no longer drinks its mother's milk.

Worms Small thin creatures that can live inside other animals and feed from them.

Further information

Books

Animals on the Farm by Sally Morgan (Franklin Watts, 1999)

Farm Animals (Eye Openers series, Dorling Kindersley, 1999)

Lamb (See How They Grow series) by Angela Royston (Dorling Kindersley, 1992)

Sheep (Farm Animals series) by Rachael Bell (Heinemann, 2000)

Sheep Farm (Let's Visit a Farm series) by Sarah Doughty & Diana Bentley (Hodder Wayland, 1990)

The Usborne Book of Farm Animals by Felicity Everett and Rachel Lockwood (Usborne, 1992)

Video

Farm Animals narrated by Johnny Morris (Dorling Kindersley)

On the Farm: Baby Animals (Dorling Kindersley)

Let's Go to the Farm/Baby Animals (Countryside Products). Visit their website at: **www.countrysidevideos.com**

Websites

www.bbc.co.uk/education/schools
BBC education online provides lots of information about animals.

www.kidsfarm.com
A fun site about the people and animals on ranches in Colorado, USA.

www.sheepusa.org
Lots of information about sheep, lambs and their wool.

Useful addresses

The National Association of Farms for Schools provides an annual directory of farms providing facilities for school visits, and an information line. To find out more write to 164, Shaftesbury Avenue, London WC2H 8HL (tel: 01422 882 708), or visit their website at: **www.farmsforschools.org.uk**

The Food and Farming Education Service provides a directory of learning resources for primary and secondary schools and a list of local resource centres. To find out more write to Stoneleigh Park, Warwickshire, CV8 2LZ (tel: 02476 535 707), or visit their website at: **www.foodandfarming.org**

Index

B
birth 4, 5, 28, 29
bottle feeding 9, 12
breeding 25, 26

C
chewing 19
coat 6, 15, 22

D
diseases 21
docking 11
drinking 7, 8, 18

F
feet 20
fields 10, 14, 18
flock 11
food 13, 16, 17

G
germs 8, 10
grass 17, 19
grazing 19

H
hay 17

L
lambing shed 4
livestock market 24,
  25

M
marking 15
mating 26, 27
meat 25
medicine 21
milk 7, 8, 9

R
rams 26

T
tagging 14
tails 10, 11
teeth 20
trough 16, 18

V
vet 20

W
water 18
weaning 12
weighing 23
wool 22
worms 21

Picture acknowledgements
Agripicture (Peter Dean) 25; Chris Fairclough Colour Library 21;
HWPL 9; Jane Upton title page, 4, 5, 6, 7, 8, 10, 11, 12, 13, 14, 15,
16, 17, 18, 19, 20, 22, 23, 24, 26, 27, 28, 29.